PEGASUS

Integrating Themes in Literature and Language

Sharing

Anthology 1

KENDALL/HUNT PUBLISHING COMPANY
2460 Kerper Boulevard P.O. Box 539 Dubuque, Iowa 52004-0539

ISBN 0–8403–7115–2

Printed in the United States of America
10 9 8 7 6 5 4 3 2 1

Table of Contents

The Adventure Begins ...

IMAGINATION, THOUGHT AND HUMOR

IMAGINATION

Imagination

Mom doesn't believe in fairies.
Dad doesn't believe in elves.
That's why they never see them
Hiding in corners and shelves.
They call it imagination.
They say it's all in my head.
That's why they don't see the brownie
That sleeps at the foot of my bed.

Bonnie Taylor

A BREAKFAST TREAT

Guess what I'm having for breakfast?
A scrambled dinosaur egg.
I'll just take it out of this basket.
It feels so warm by my leg.

But wait! I can see the shell cracking.
I see a small head and it's cute!
Now for breakfast I'm having some corn flakes,
And my dinosaur's having some fruit!

Sandra Liatsos

Get out of my room, monster.
Get away from my stuff.
I'm big and strong and you should know
I'm really, really tough.
Get out of my room, monster,
I can yell and scream.
I'll close my eyes, then open wide,
I know you're not a dream.

Get out of my room, monster.
I really don't like you.
This room is mine; I know it.
It's not big enough for two.
These are my blankets, monster.
This is my bat and ball.
Along with everything else you see,
hanging on the wall.

This is my own room, monster,
And I don't want to share.
I better not see you pop right down
and sit upon my chair.
I still can see you, monster,
Sticking out from under my bed.
I see your bright eyes shining,
yellow, yellow . . . RED.

I don't like you, monster.
I said GO AWAY!
Wait a minute, monster.
What did you try to say?
Oh, Kitty. Is that really you?
You gave me quite a fright,
Never mind, Kitty, go to sleep now.
Good Night, Good Night, Good Night!

Rita Milios

MONSTER MOVIE

The monster movie was a fright
For anyone to see.
I shivered and I hollered
And I screamed in agony.
I tried to watch the monsters fight.
Sometimes I didn't dare.
Sometimes I shut my eyes and hid
Underneath my chair.

Sandra Liatsos

MY KITE IS UP A TREE

My kite is up a tree again.
I cannot get it down.
It always has to flip and dive
And act just like a clown.
I wish I had a ladder
To climb and set it free,
Or a dinosaur who
could use his teeth
To bite it down to me.

Sandra Liatsos

Christopher and the Dinosaur

When Christopher went to the library, he got a book about dinosaurs. And from that day on Christopher talked about dinosaurs, thought about dinosaurs, drew pictures of dinosaurs, saw movies about dinosaurs.

But Christopher wanted to see a REAL dinosaur.

"You can't see a <u>real</u> dinosaur," said Christopher's mother. "Dinosaurs lived millions of years ago. There aren't any dinosaurs now."

"There might be a dinosaur SOMEWHERE," Christopher said.

Christopher looked for a dinosaur
on his grandfather's farm,
at the park,
in his own back yard.
But he couldn't find a dinosaur . . .

UNTIL

One night when the moon was full,
and a soft breeze rustled the apple tree,
something woke Christopher up.

Scrape, Scratch, SNORT!
SOMETHING was outside his window.

Something BIG!

There in the moonlight was a dinosaur!
Its tail s t r e t c h e d
from the front of Christopher's house
clear back to his bedroom. The dinosaur's
head bumped the TV antenna up on the roof.

The dinosaur had a wide, flat, mouth
like the bill of a duck.
It was an Anatosaurus,
the duck-billed dinosaur!

"Hi, Anatosaurus!" Christopher called.

Anatosaurus thumped his huge tail.
All the apples fell off the tree.
Christopher giggled,
although he knew he shouldn't.

"Look what you did, Anatosaurus!"

Anatosaurus snorted. He rubbed his back against Christopher's house.

Scrape! Scratch!

Chips of paint flew in all directions.

``Let ME scratch your back,'' Christopher said.

Christopher got a ladder and a yard broom. He scratched the ruffle of skin that ran down the dinosaur's back. He scratched the billions of bumps on the dinosaur's leathery hide.

Anatosaurus hissed contentedly.
His tail swung back and forth.
It knocked over the lawn chairs,
and the umbrella table,
and got tangled in the telephone wires.

"PLEASE watch your tail, Anatosaurus!"
said Christopher.

Anatosaurus scooped a mouthful of water lilies from the neighbor's fish pond.
Christopher scrambled down the ladder.

"Mrs. Jones isn't going to like that!"

"Snort," said Anatosaurus.
He spit out eight water lilies and three gold fish.

``Not THAT, Anatosaurus!'' yelled Christopher.

``Snort,'' said Anatosaurus. He stopped chewing the tulip bulbs Christopher's mother had planted.

``I'll find you something to eat.''

Anatosaurus shook his tail
and headed toward the shopping center.
"STOP! SIT! STAY!" Christopher shouted.

But the dinosaur had spotted something,
and he charged straight for it.
Anatosaurus crashed through the window
of the pet store.
Christopher covered his eyes
and peeked through his fingers.
He saw the dinosaur scoop out a mouthful
of green plants from an aquarium.
CRUNCH! MUNCH!
Anatosaurus ground up the plants
like a lawn mower.

PET STORE

Then Anatosaurus started on the fish bowls. But, he got his bill stuck.

WHAM! SLAM! BAM!

The kitten box spilled into the puppy pen. The monkey cage crashed into the rabbit hutch. The rabbit hutch toppled onto the parrot perch. The door of the snake cage flew open, and all the snakes crawled into the aisle.

HISS!

SQUAWK!

CHATTER!

ARF!

SPIT! PSSSSSSSST!

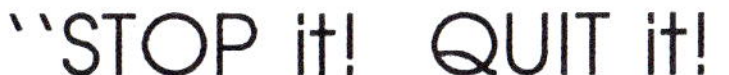

"STOP it! QUIT it!
Get OUT of there!" Christopher screamed.

Anatosaurus stood up on his hind feet.
The roof of the pet store went with him.
About this time the first police car arrived
with its red lights blinking
and its siren shrieking.

Christopher waved his arms.

"RUN, Anatosaurus! DON'T let them CATCH you!"

The last time Christopher saw Anatosaurus, the big dinosaur was lumbering down the street with the police cars far behind him.

From that day to this—
Christopher still talks about dinosaurs,
draws pictures of dinosaurs,
reads books about dinosaurs,
sees movies about dinosaurs.

But when the moon is full and a soft breeze rustles the apple tree,
Christopher always tiptoes to his window because he knows that SOMEWHERE out there. . . .

THERE IS A REAL DINOSAUR!

MONSTER

I saw him in a nightmare.
His wide, jagged jaws.
He lunged and grabbed
The giant rocks
And did not stop to pause.
I smile to think
He haunted me
In the dark of night.
By day he's just
A steam shovel
At a nearby building site.

Sandra Liatsos

Galumph

Here comes a dinosaur,
Galumph, galumph.
An early riser,
Galumph, galumph.
Through the mud,
Galumph, galumph.
He rolls like a tub,
Galumph, galumph.
Into the water,
Galumph, galumph.
The dinosaur totters,
Galumph, galumph.
To eat a lily . . .
He looks pretty silly.

Sherry B. Hanson

A LOOK AT LIZARDS

Dinosaurs no longer roam the earth, but did you know that there are almost 3,000 different types of lizards that do? All lizards are cold-blooded reptiles, but not all lizards are alike. Some lizards can do some pretty amazing things!

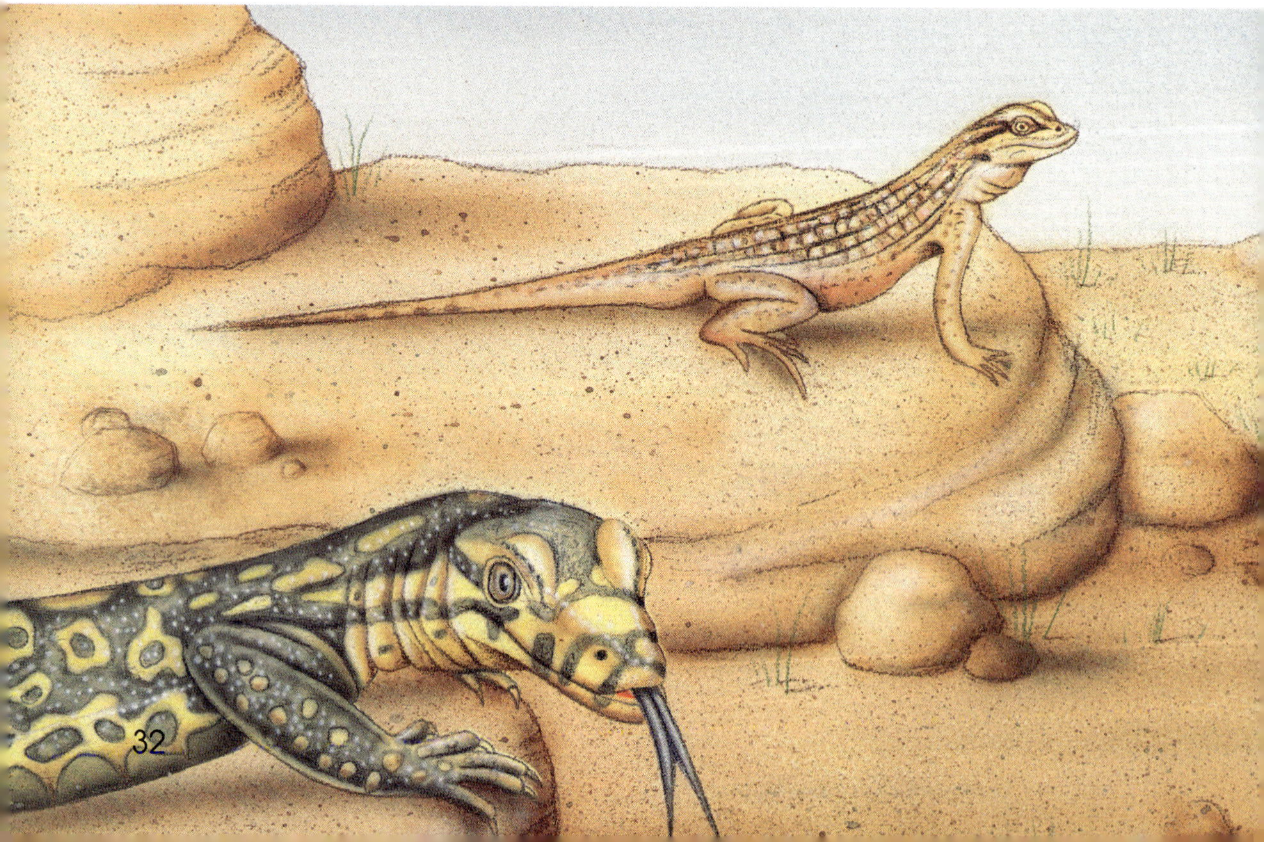

Did you know that many lizards escape from enemies by dropping their tails? That's right. If they get caught by their tail, it breaks off. But don't worry. It doesn't hurt, and the lizard soon grows a new tail.

Geckos are lizards that can walk straight up walls. They can walk across ceilings, too. They can even cling to smooth surfaces like glass without falling off. Geckos have special pads on the bottom of their feet. The special pads have lots of tiny hooks on them. These pads help geckos cling to almost any surface.

Basilisks are fast runners. These lizards stand on their back legs when they are frightened. Basilisks move so quickly that they run right on top of the water.

Frilled lizards live in Australia. Folds of loose skin grow around this lizard's neck. When the frilled lizard is frightened, the skin puffs up like a huge collar. Then the frilled lizard bares its teeth and tries to scare away its enemies.

The draco is another lizard with loose folds of skin. But the skin is along each side of the draco's thin body rather than around its neck. Dracos don't use this skin to scare away enemies. They use it to fly from tree to tree. When dracos are ready to go to a different tree, they simply jump into the air. The loose skin spreads out like colorful wings.

Huge marine iguanas are lizards who live by the sea. They are found near the Galapagos Islands. These angry looking iguanas puff steam through their noses to scare away unwanted visitors.

Gila monsters are one of the few types of poisonous lizards. You can tell when a Gila monster is hungry by looking at its tail. Gila monsters store food in their tails. When they have finished eating, their tails grow big and fat. Can you guess what it means if the Gila monster's tail is thin?

Did you know that a horned toad is actually a type of lizard? Horned toads try to run away if they're frightened. But if they can't escape, they know what to do. They shoot a stream of blood from the corner of each eye. This doesn't hurt, but it certainly is scary. The enemy is the one who runs away!

Chameleons are lizards that change colors. If the chameleon is angry or frightened, it might change color. Changes in temperature or the amount of sunlight might also cause chameleons to change color. Changing colors helps these lizards remain safe as they blend in with their surroundings.

You've never seen a real dinosaur, but have you ever seen any of these lizards? Learning about lizards is fun because there are so many different kinds and they do such interesting things!

FRIENDS AND FAMILY

FRIENDSHIP

THE MORE WE GET TOGETHER

The more we get together, together, together,
The more we get together, the happier we'll be.
'Cause your friends are my friends
and my friends are your friends.
The more we get together
the happier we'll be.

UP WITH PUPPIES

Puppies wiggle.
Puppies glow.
Puppies eat.
Puppies grow.
Puppies play.
Puppies nap.
Puppies warm up
Someone's lap.
Their fur is soft.
Their legs are short.
I love MY puppy.
I call him Sport.

Gail Minthorn

Juan and Maria Are Best Friends

Juan and Maria were best friends. They did everything together. They shared their lunches. They shared their books. They even shared a baseball.

One day a new kid moved in across the hall. His name was Mark. Mark was the same age as Juan and Maria.

Mark walked to school by himself his first day. He tried to catch up to Juan and Maria. But they would not wait. They were best friends.

Mark tried to sit with Juan and Maria at lunch. But they moved away. They were best friends.

After school, Mark wanted to play baseball with Juan and Maria. He watched and he waited. Maria threw the ball too hard. Juan missed it. The ball bounced and bounced. Then it rolled and rolled. Juan and Maria looked and could not find it.

But Mark had been watching and waiting. He saw where the ball had gone. Mark picked up the ball and gave it to Maria.

Now Mark, Juan and Maria do everything together. They share their lunches. They share their books. They even share a baseball. They are best friends.

BEST FRIENDS

My best friend takes care of ME.
She hugs me lots.
She's never mean.
She feeds me well.
And keeps me clean.

My best friend is fun for ME.
She makes me laugh.
She skips and sings.
We dance along,
And swing on swings.

My best friend is nice to ME.
She does not lie.
She's kind and good.
She never yells
And says, ''You should!''
My best friend is ME.

Phyllis Droesch

Tommy Bear

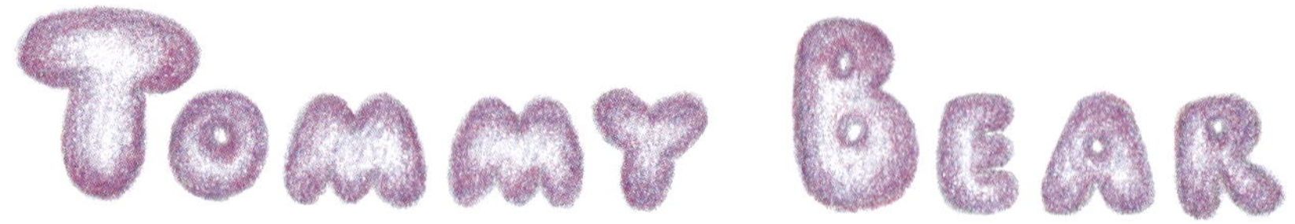

Tommy Bear's my special friend
He's old and worn and brown.
But he's always there to be with me
When others aren't around.

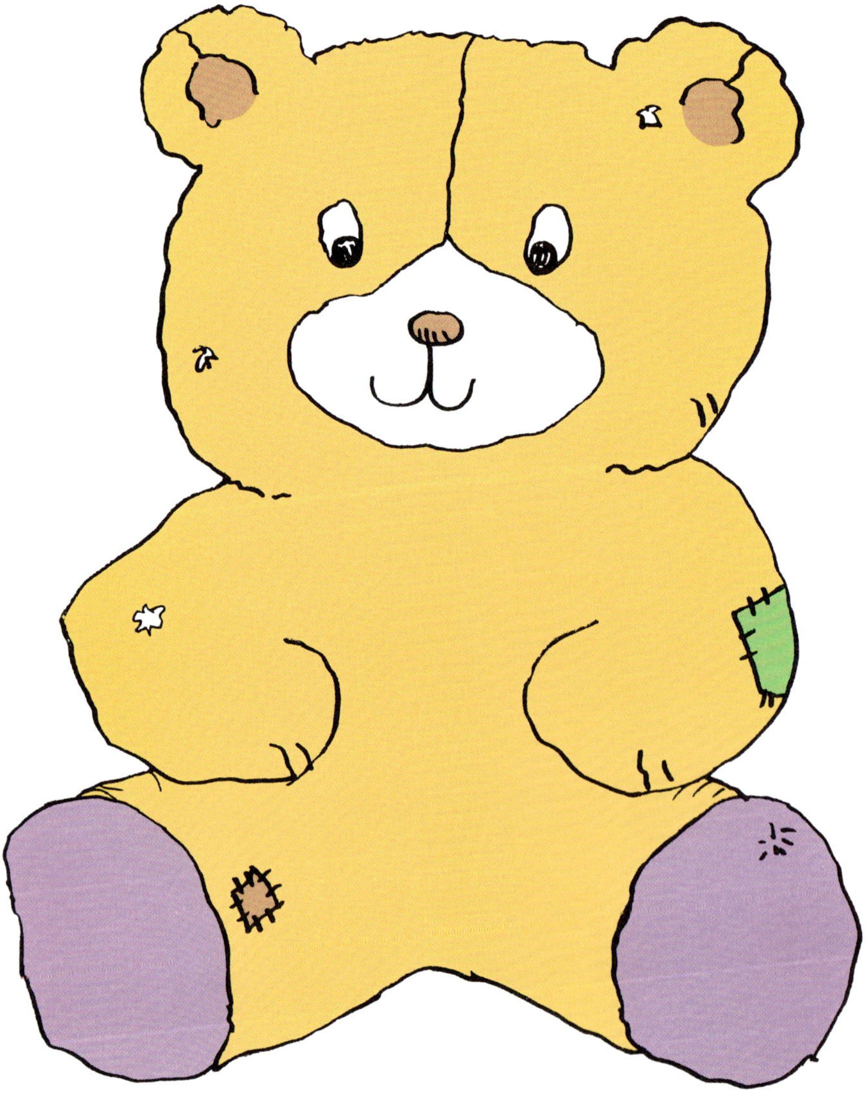

When I feel all sickly
And Mom puts me right to bed,
Tommy stays there with me
On my pillow, by my head.

And when I'm really scared sometimes
From something on T.V.
I reach out for my Tommy
And he's always there for me!

When I see something happen
That makes me feel all sad,
I hold on to my Tommy
And it doesn't seem so bad!

And when I get in trouble
For not doing what I should,
I hold on to my Tommy
And he makes me feel so good.

Tommy Bear's my special friend
He's old and worn and brown
He's always there to be with me
When others aren't around.

Barbara Saul

MONKEYSHINES

Monkey, monkey, monkey, me.
Monkey swinging in a tree.
Monkey grunt, monkey grin.
Monkey says, ''Come on, join in.''
Monkey one, monkey two,
Play monkey see and monkey do.
Monkey me, monkey who?
Monkey, monkey, monkey, YOU!

Sydnie Kleinhenz

Dear Yoshi

Around the world,
across the sea.
I write to you.
You write to me.

September 8

Dear Yoshi,
How are you?
School just started.
The lunch room was crazy today. Tanya brought a frog.
Your pen pal, Jill

November 22

Dear Jill,
Today was my turn to help clean the room after school. I played like I was a Samurai Warrior.

Your friend,
Yoshi

Around the world,
across the sea.
I write to you.
You write to me.

February 15

Dear Yoshi,
How are you doing? I saved my allowance for a new video game but my brother wrecked it!
Write back soon,
Your pen pal, Jill

May 17

Dear Jill,
Children's Festival was yesterday. What a great time! We got our own money to spend any way we wanted to. I bought a kite shaped like a fish.

Your friend,
Yoshi

Around the world,
across the sea.
I write to you.
You write to me.

June 4

Dear Yoshi,

School's out! Will you go on vacation this summer? I get to go to the Grand Canyon next week. I might ride a burro down to the bottom.

your pen pal, Jill

P.S. I'll send you a postcard

July 3

Dear Jill,

For vacation, I get to zoom on the bullet train to see my grandparents. Then I go to Mt. Aso. I sure hope the volcano doesn't erupt while we're there.

Your friend,
Yoshi

Around the world,

across the sea.

I write to you.

You write to me.

August 21

Dear Yoshi,

Guess what? I'm coming to your house! Mom has a meeting in Japan. I'll see you in December. I can hardly wait!

Your pen pal, Jill

Around the world,
across the sea.
I visit you.
You visit me.

ENVIRONMENT

WEATHER

A RAINBOW

I saw a rainbow
Striped with blue,
Gold and green,
And orange, too.
I wished the rainbow
Was a slide.
I wanted to
Ride down its side.

Sandra Liatsos

FOUR SEASONS

Spring is showery, flowery, bowery.
Summer . . . hoppy, croppy, poppy.
Autumn . . . wheezy, sneezy, freezy.
Winter . . . slippy, drippy, nippy.

Anonymous

IN THE SIZZLING SUMMER SUN

I see the brightness of the day,
I want to run and leap and play,
In the sizzling summer sun.

I see the green leaves on the trees,
I feel the brushing of the breeze,
In the sizzling summer sun.

I feed a bird a bit of bread,
I watch it peck and bob its head,
In the sizzling summer sun.

I like big bugs, they're fun to see,
I don't think they will bother me,
In the sizzling summer sun.

I kneel down low upon my knees,
I watch the worms and bees,
In the sizzling summer sun.

I like the shade tree for a rest,
I look up high, a squirrel's nest,
In the sizzling summer sun.

I squirt the water on my feet,
I feel the cool instead of heat,
In the sizzling summer sun.

It's fun to do these things, you see,
So won't you come and play with me?
In the sizzling summer sun.

Mickey Dowdy

RAINBOW

I saw a rainbow in the sky
And wondered how it reached so high,
And how, suspended in the air,
It made a bridge from here to there.

Sandra Liatsos

WIND PONY

Galloping, galloping over the hill,
Wind is a pony who never is still.
He's whistling
  under the windows and door,
And twirling the trees
  till they rollick and roar.
He's soaring and sailing
  and neighing delight,
And trying to carry me up like a kite.

Sandra Liatsos

KITES

By Robin Brown Age 6 1/2

How Kites sail
HIGH......
Breezing and wheezing
Into the sky.
How I love kites.
They're pretty and bitty.
But they are not good
To fly in the city.

GOOD-BYE......

Library
childrens
Park
Robin's
Hotel
& shop
Kelly's
Diner
Hats

WIND VANE EXPERIMENT

You will need:

1. Glue the spool to the cardboard.

2. Cut a slot in the straw.

3. Put the arrow in the slot.

4. Tape the arrow to the straw.
5. Put the straw in the spool.

6. Set it outside in the wind.

Question:

Which way is the wind blowing?

WEATHER OR NOT!

(Jokes About the Weather)

by Diane Burns and Andy Burns

1. Where do weathermen save their money?

   In cloudbanks

2. What two letters of the alphabet describe a blizzard?

   I C (icy)

3. How do weathermen bounce a basketball?

   They drizzle it.

4. What is a weatherman's favorite breakfast drink?

   Tornado (tomato) juice

5. How can you tell if a tropical storm is friendly?

   When the tidal waves

6. What animals are a weatherman's favorite pet?

   B-lizards

7. What kind of bedding does a weatherman hang on his laundry line?

   Sleets (sheets) and fog-blankets

8. Why do snowclouds move fast?

   Because they are always in a flurry

Melanie sat in the reading circle. She did not know what the story was about. She did not listen to the other children read. She was watching the sky turn black.

Her teacher stood up. ``Everyone line up at the door,'' Mrs. Wright said. She opened the windows a little bit.

Melanie and the other children walked out to the hall. They faced the wall and got down on their knees. Melanie put her arms over her head and curled up into a ball.

Melanie heard a loud roar. She heard glass breaking. Her arms tightened around her head. Soon the roar stopped.

"We can all get up now," Mrs. Wright said. "The storm is over. You did a fine job listening and moving quickly but carefully. We are all safe because we did the right thing."

Mrs. Wright was proud of her class. They had practiced this before and now they knew what to do.

Melanie knew what to do during a tornado at school. What things can you do when you know a tornado is coming?

1. If you are outside, find a ditch or some other low place.
2. If you are downtown, go to the lowest part of a newer building. Crouch down next to a wall and stay away from windows. Do not go to large open rooms like a gymnasium or a movie theater.
3. If you are home, go to the lowest level of your house. Go to your basement or a small room away from windows. A closet or under stairs are good places to wait.

KEEP OUT

PERSONAL FEELINGS AND GROWTH

PERSONAL GROWTH

WHEN I GROW UP

When I grow up . . .

I'll eat ice cream for breakfast,
And cookies for lunch
I won't brush my teeth
Or take a bath.
I'll stay up all night long
And won't take a nap.

I'll jump on the couch
And ride my bike in the house.
I'll go outside without a hat,
And I'll buy a mouse for a pet.
I'll play in the dirt
And I'll climb every tree—YOU'LL SEE.
I'll do just what I want . . .
  When I grow up!

Rita Milios

What Bear Did Best

Bear had many friends in the forest. Everyone liked Bear. But one day something made Bear sad.

``I'm not good at anything,'' said Bear. ``I'm big and slow!''

"Maybe I can fly like you," said Bear to Owl.

Bear took a long running jump and landed flat on his stomach.

"I can't fly," said Bear.

Bear saw Rabbit hopping quickly through the woods.

"I can hop like Rabbit," said Bear.

Bear tried to hop, but he was too big to hop very high. He bumped his toe on a tree root and sat with a thump on the ground.

''Ug,'' said Bear, catching his breath. ''I can't hop very well either. I wonder what I can do best.''

Bear saw Squirrel jumping from tree to tree. ''I wonder. . . .'' said Bear.

``No,'' said Owl, ``You could hurt yourself. Everyone is good at something. Just wait. You will find out what you do best.''

Just then, Mother Bluebird cried, ``Help! Help! A tree branch is breaking. It is right over my babies' nest. If it falls, it will hurt them.''

``I can help,'' said Bear.

He climbed up into the tree. With his strong arms, he lifted the tree branch away from the baby birds.

"Oh, Bear, thank you," said Mother Bluebird.

"I'm big and strong and I can climb trees. I don't have to fly or hop. Now I know what I do best," said Bear.

THINKING ABOUT MY BODY

I'm lucky that my nose
knows just what to do.
I'm lucky that my feet
know their lessons, too.
Imagine if my nose
walked right off my face,
or if my feet began to sneeze
all over the place.
Imagine if my ears
gobbled down my dinner
and my belly began to sing,
I might become much thinner.
I could worry about my every
crazy mixed-up part.
I'm lucky that my body
is so very, very smart!

Sandra Liatsos

YUM-M-M
DO-RE-MI
Ah-
Choooooooo.....

Who are you?

Ryan Bryan sneaked out of bed. He ran after Silky, the cat. He jumped off the high kitchen stool. He turned cartwheels in the big front room.

''What a silly GOOSE you are,'' said Mother.

''I'm not a GOOSE,'' said Ryan Bryan. ''I don't have white feathers. I don't have a long yellow beak. I don't go 'HONK HONK'!''

Ryan Bryan dressed in old blue jeans. He ate pancakes with sweet maple syrup. He gulped down a huge glass of milk.

``What a big PIG you are,'' said sister Cindy.

``I'm not a PIG,'' said Ryan Bryan. ``I don't have pink skin. I don't have a curly tail. I don't go `OINK OINK'!''

Ryan Bryan ran out to play. He climbed on his new red bike. He splashed through a puddle. He got all wet.

''What a MONKEY you are,'' said his brother Peter.

''I'm not a MONKEY,'' said Ryan Bryan. I don't live in the jungle. I don't swing through the trees. I don't go 'SCREECH SCREECH'!''

Ryan Bryan played hide-and-go-seek. He hid from Gramps behind the barn door. He crawled up on a bale of hay. "Boo!" he cried, when Gramps came in.

"What a TIGER you are," said Gramps.

"I'm not a TIGER," said Ryan Bryan. "I don't have black stripes. I don't have long whiskers. I don't go 'ROARRR ROARRR'!"

Ryan Bryan ate his supper. He ate a hot dog with pickles. He drank pink lemonade. He had chocolate ice cream.

''Time for pajamas,'' said Mother.''

''Time to brush your teeth,'' said Cindy.

''Time to pick up your toys,'' said Peter.

''Time for a story,'' said Gramps.

''Time for bed,'' said Father.

"I DON'T WANT TO GO TO BED!" said Ryan Bryan.

"What a BEAR you are," said Father.

"I'm not a BEAR," said Ryan Bryan. "I don't have fuzzy brown fur. I don't have sharp claws. I don't go 'GRRR GRRR'!"

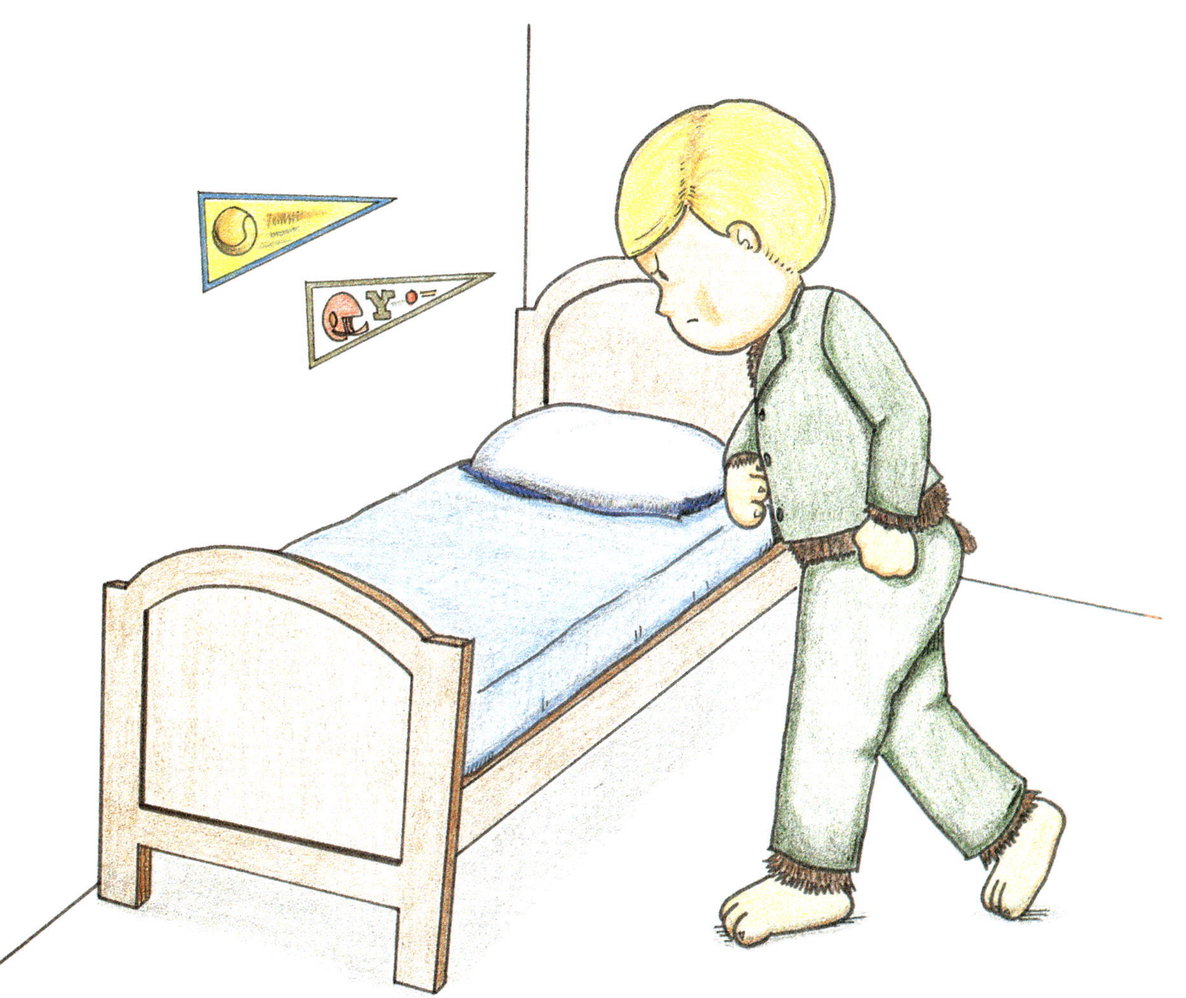

``If you are not a BEAR,'' said Father, ``who are you?''

``If you are not a TIGER,'' said Gramps, ``who are you?''

``If you are not a MONKEY,'' said Peter, ``who are you?''

``If you are not a PIG,'' said Cindy, ``who are you?''

``And if you are not a silly GOOSE,'' said Mother, ``who are you?''

"Yes," they all said at once.

"WHO ARE YOU?"

"DON'T YOU KNOW?" said Ryan Bryan. "I'm just ME!"

WINK

I really wish
that I could wink.
It's something fun
to do, I think.
But, when I try,
I only blink—
Oh why, oh why,
can't I wink?
Then one day
a big surprise,
I close just <u>one</u>,
not <u>both</u> my eyes.
I did a wink,
I think, I think.
I think I did
a wink . . .
WOW!

Joan Bransfield Graham

SKIN

Such a useful thing
. . . my skin,
it won't let out
what must stay IN.

It lets my mouth
make funny faces
and keeps my ears
in both their places.

If I didn't have
. . . a skin,
what kind of shape
would I be IN?

Joan Bransfield Graham

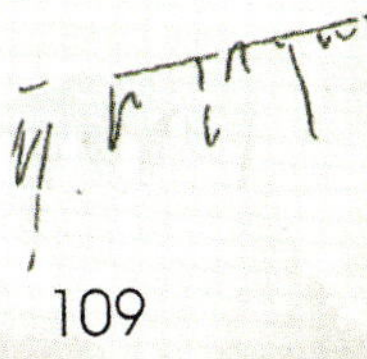

MORGAN'S MOVING DAY

Morgan was moving away from Youngstown. His dad was being transferred to another company.

This made Morgan sad. He had to leave his school, his neighborhood, and his friends.

The last day of school, Morgan said good-bye to his classmates and to his teacher. He would miss them.

On his way home from school, Morgan stopped at Grandma Wakefield's house.

``Grandma, I'm leaving tomorrow and I'll miss you.''

``I know Morgan, and I'm going to miss you too. I made you some cookies to take on your long trip.''

"Morgan, here's a postcard with my address and stamp on it. You write me a message and put your new address on it so we can stay in touch."

"Thank you Grandma, I promise to write."

The next morning, Morgan's best friend, Tony, told him good-bye. They took one last look at the tree house in the backyard where they played so often.

They watched as the last piece of furniture was placed on the moving van. They watched as Dad put the last box into the van.

Morgan, here's a postcard with my address and stamp on it. You write me a message and put your new address on it so we can stay in touch.

``Thank you Tony, I'll miss you.''

``I'll miss you too, Morgan.''

After a long trip, Morgan arrived at his new house. Everything seemed so strange.

``Hi folks,'' shouted a friendly voice from across the fence. ``Are you the new neighbors?''

``Yes, we are. We're Madelyn and Joe and this is our son, Morgan.''

We're the Franklins. Morgan, we have a grandson your age that comes to visit and I have a feeling that you're going to become good friends.''

That night Morgan called Tony and told him about his new home and the people he'd met. Next morning, Morgan wrote a message on the postcard and mailed it to Grandma. It was going to be fun having a pen pal.

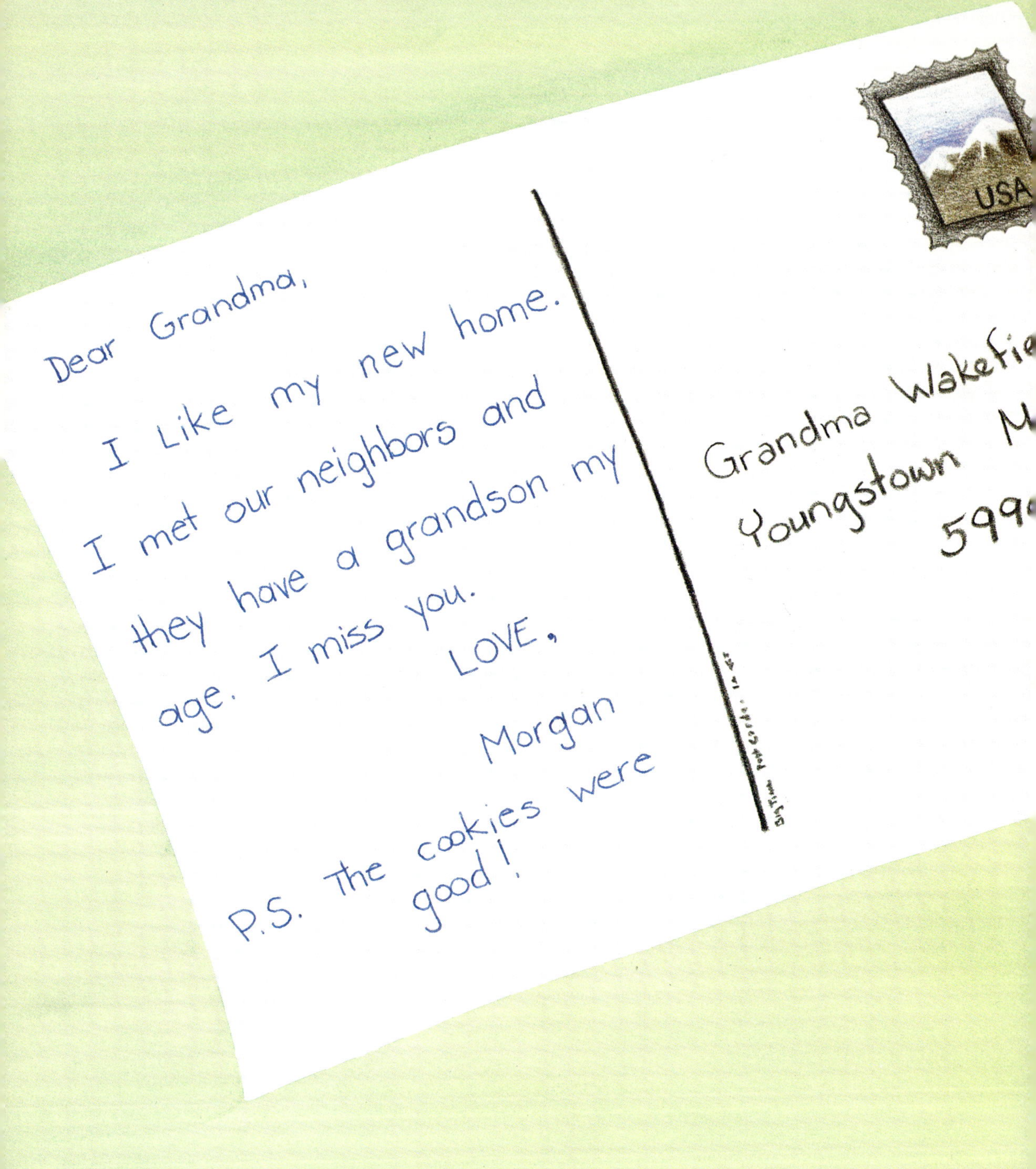

Dear Grandma,

I Like my new home. I met our neighbors and they have a grandson my age. I miss you.

LOVE,

Morgan

P.S. The cookies were good!

Grandma Wakefie
Youngstown M
599

USA

Morgan rushed home on his bike to meet his new friend. This place was going to be A-OK.

A NEW BROTHER

I feel like laughing, and hopping, and singing,
I feel that all kinds of bells should be ringing.
My new baby brother was born in the night,
With ten toes, ten fingers, everything right.
A brand new person I will love and can hold,
It's so wonderful . . . all the world should be told.

Ruth Cox Anderson

Lydia the Little One

Lydia was six years old. Her brother Levi was ten years old. Lydia didn't like being the little one. She couldn't do everything she wanted to do. She wasn't allowed to do the things that Levi could do.

Whenever Lydia asked her mother if she could do something special, her mother always said, ``No, Lydia, you're too little to do that!'' even though Lydia didn't think she was.

Whenever Lydia asked her father if she could do something special, her father always said, ``No, Lydia, you're too little to do that!'' even though Lydia didn't think she was.

Whenever Lydia's mother or father would tell her, ''No,'' she would always say, ''But Levi gets to do that.''

''Levi is older,'' her mother and father would both say.

''That's not fair!'' Lydia would tell them.

''I'm sorry,'' her mother and father would say as they would shake their heads a little. Then they would go back to what they were doing.

They didn't care that she was the little one. They didn't care that she couldn't do things. It made Lydia angry. It made Lydia angry that they always said "No" and that they didn't care. It made Lydia so-o-o-o angry, that sometimes she screamed a little when they told her, "No." Not all the time. She didn't scream all the time. But sometimes she did.

Lydia wanted to stay up late on a school night to watch the special show on television that ended at nine o'clock.

She couldn't.

Levi could.

Lydia wanted to walk to the library all by herself and check out some books and walk back home all by herself, too.

She couldn't

Levi could.

Lydia wanted to walk down to the little grocery store on Fourth Street all by herself and bring back something her mother needed.

She couldn't.

Levi could.

Lydia wanted to use her father's real hammer and saw while her father was at work, instead of the pretend tools.

She couldn't.

Levi could.

Lydia wanted to be dropped off at the YMCA to go swimming with her friends and then call when she was ready to come home.

She couldn't.

Levi could.

Then one day, after

many

many

many

many

many

''NO's!!''

Lydia could stay up late on a school night to watch the special show on television that ended at nine o'clock.

Lydia could walk to the library all by herself and check out some books and walk back home all by herself, too.

Lydia could walk down to the little grocery store on Fourth Street all by herself and bring back something her mother needed.

Lydia could use her father's real hammer and saw while her father was at work, instead of the pretend tools.

Lydia could be dropped off at the YMCA to go swimming with her friends and then call when she was ready to come home.

And pretty soon, after

many

many

many

many

many

other ``NO's!!'' Lydia could do lots and lots and lots of other new and special things.

YESTERDAY

EARLY SETTLERS

Legend Of The Sleeping Ute

Once there was a very old Ute Indian chief. He had grown very tired and thought it was time to take a rest. He decided to take a very, very long nap.

His nap might last many days.

It might last many months.

It might last many years.

His people were afraid. Their chief had never done anything like this before. He had always been with them. What if there was trouble while he napped? What if their enemies came? The people didn't know what to do without their chief. They all looked worried.

The chief smiled.

"Do not be afraid," he said. "I will wake up if you need me." The people nodded and smiled. Then they laughed. How silly they had been. If they needed their chief, all they had to do was to wake him.

So the old Ute Indian chief went up on the mountain. He wanted a soft bed to sleep in, but there wasn't one on the mountain. He had an idea. He started grabbing the clouds that were floating past the mountain.

When he had gathered enough, he started packing them into his pockets. He had many pockets all over his clothes. The full pockets made him very puffy. He knew he would have a fine bed to lay in now. Then he folded his arms in front of him and went to sleep.

Many years have passed since the Indian chief went up to the top of the mountain. The people still know they can call him if they need him.

Sometimes when the Ute Indians look up at the mountains they smile and laugh. They see many clouds moving around the top of the mountain. They know their chief just rolled over in his sleep and clouds have fallen from his pockets.

If you live near mountains, you might see clouds gathered around the top. Maybe there is an Indian chief sleeping up there, too.

A Legend of MAIZE

In times long ago, when the Chippewa Indians hunted for most of their food, there grew a boy who wanted to help other people. The young Chippewa boy took many walks by himself to think about what he might do for others.

One day, as the boy walked, he thought about the Great Spirit and the beautiful earth he had made. He prayed to the Great Spirit. He prayed for the Great Spirit to show him how he could help others.

As the boy was praying, a young man appeared to him. He was dressed in a green robe. He wore green plumes on his head.

"The Great Spirit has sent me," said the young man dressed in green. His voice sounded like breezes rustling the grass.

"I have a job for you, but first I must test your strength. Wrestle with me."

They quickly became friends. They wrestled together for a long time. Then the friend left. The boy laid down to rest.

The next day the friend in green returned. They wrestled again. This time the boy grew stronger as he struggled with his friend. This happened again the next day. Each time the boy grew stronger.

``Tomorrow I will come once more,'' said the friend in green. You have become strong enough to go back and help your people. I will give you a gift tomorrow and you may take it back with you.

The next day the young man appeared again. They wrestled one last time. Then the young man handed the boy a bag full of seeds. He told the boy to use his new strength to plant the seeds. He told him to keep the ground moist and keep away the weeds.

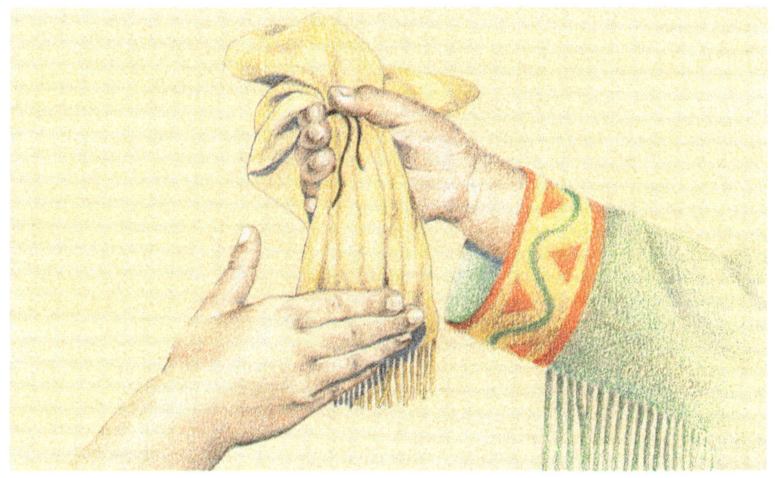

"After many days of caring for these seeds, you will think I have come again to see you, for the ground will be green, just as I am, and filled with green plumes, just as I am. These plants are called Maize and if you tend them well you will harvest much food from them." Then the young man left.

The boy thought about what his friend had said. The young man was from the Great Spirit, so he must do as he had been told.

The boy returned to his home. He planted the bag of seeds in the ground. He used his new strength and watered the soil. He pulled out weed sprouts every day.

Soon green plumes rose out of the soil. They spread into broad leaves. In autumn the plants were tall and golden.

His people were able to harvest the grain to make food. They were also able to keep seeds from the grain to plant again. They knew, with their strength to care for the plants, they would always have enough food.

This is how Maize was given to all Indians.

The Money Tree
(An Apache Legend)

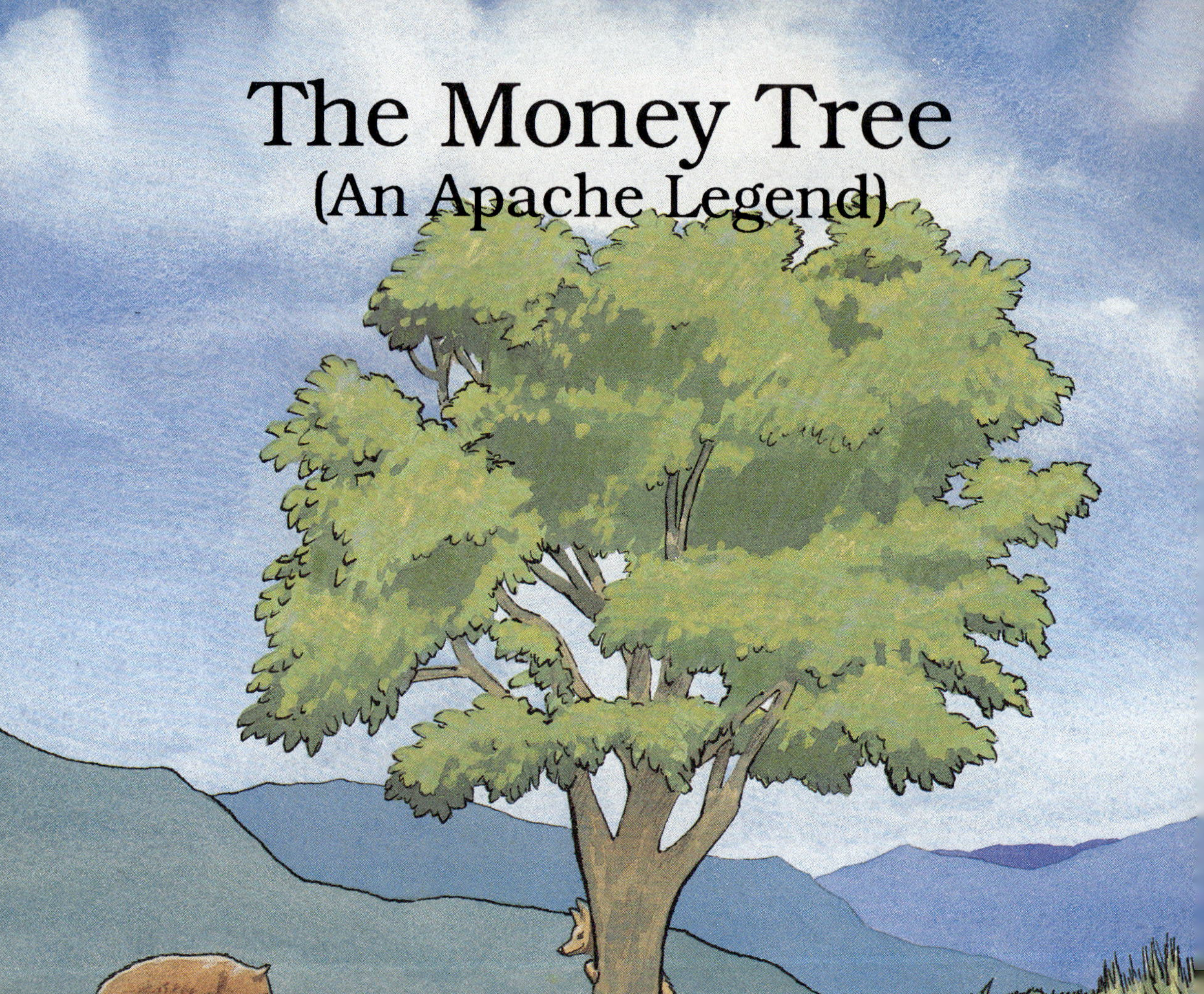

Long, long ago, the Coyote and the Bear did not like each other. Coyote was always being silly and playing tricks on Bear. Bear never liked the tricks. Bear liked to stay home and count his money, for he had lots of money.

One day Coyote saw Bear counting his money. Bear loved money and always wanted more. He kept his money in a big box. Coyote wanted some of Bear's money. He thought, ''How can I get it?'' He thought and thought. Then he had a good idea.

Coyote found a big tree. He put his last ten coins up in the tree. Then he waited for Bear. Soon, Bear came by.

"Good day, Bear!" said Coyote. "What do you have in your fine box?"

``I have my money in here,'' said Bear.

``Oh, how nice,'' answered Coyote. ``I don't need money myself. I have a money tree.'' Bear looked at the tree.

``Is this your money tree?'' Bear asked. Then Bear laughed. He said, ``Coyote, you made that up! No one has a money tree.''

"I will show you," said Coyote. Then he shook the tree. A few coins fell down. Coyote shook the tree again. A few more coins fell down. They were the coins that Coyote had put in the tree. Of course, Bear did not know that.

Bear said, "You are right, Coyote! It is a money tree and I want it. Then I will have lots and lots of money. Will you sell the tree? Please, please sell me your money tree! I will give you all the money in this box."

Coyote shook his head. "You don't want this tree, Bear. I think we have all its money."

But Bear would not listen to Coyote. Bear asked and asked.

At last Coyote said, ``OK, Bear. I will sell you this tree.''

Bear gave Coyote all the money in the box. Coyote took the money and laughed all the way home.

After Coyote left, Bear wanted to see more money fall from the tree. He shook it hard. Nothing happened. Bear shook it again. No money fell down.

Bear said, "Coyote was right. The money is all gone. But I will wait for more to grow."

And he sat down and waited
and waited
and waited.

Chapter 1—About the Indians

Long ago, before white men found America, other people lived here. They are called Native Americans or Indians. They took good care of the land. They only took the things they needed to make their food, homes and clothes. They thought the land belonged to everyone.

They told many stories to their children and friends, but never wrote them down. They did not have letters or an alphabet. The Indians, or Native Americans, did not have horses either. It was hard for them to go from place to place. After the Native Americans got horses from the white men, life changed for some of them.

The Native Americans lived in groups called tribes. There were many, many tribes that lived in different parts of America. The tribes spoke different languages and wore different kinds of clothes. They wore their hair in different ways. They also had different kinds of work. Some were farmers and some were hunters. They lived in many different ways.

Chapter 2—Northeast Indians

The tribes that were part of the Northeast Indians lived in the woodlands of the Northeastern United States.

They hunted for some of their food and grew some of their food. They made their clothes from deerskin.

They didn't have to move to find their food so they lived in one place. These places were called villages. They made their houses in the villages and covered them with bark. These houses were called "long houses." A long house is like an apartment. Many people lived in each long house.

The Northeast Indians made beads from clam shells. They made many things with the beads. They made strings, belts and pictures. They also used beads like money.

Northeast Indians also made masks. They called them False Face masks. They thought they needed the masks to keep people well. They believed there were horrible heads without bodies that could make people sick. They wore the masks to break the spell and scare away the horrible heads.

Chapter 3—Southeast Indians

The tribes that were part of the Southeast Indians lived in the southeast part of the United States. An Indian from a Southeast tribe made the first Indian alphabet.

These tribes grew lots of corn to use for many things. They also grew most of their other food too. They lived in houses in towns. Some tribes lived in houses called ``chickees.'' A chickee is on a high floor or platform. A chickee has open walls to keep the Indians cool because it can be very warm in the south.

Some of the men tattooed their bodies. When they did great things they got a special design for their tattoo. The women didn't want tattoos. Instead, they wanted cloth to make bright, colored dresses.

Chapter 4—Plains Indians

The tribes that were part of the Plains Indians lived in the central plains of the United States and Canada.

They gathered plants and roots for their food. They also hunted buffalo. They hunted with bows and arrows. Horses were very important for hunting and moving across the plains.

The buffalo moved about on the plains. If the Plains Indians wanted food, they had to follow the buffalo. They had to have homes that could be moved. They lived in teepees. They used 10 to 15 buffalo skins sewn together to make a teepee. They painted pictures on the outside of their teepees.

The Indians wore clothes made from buffalo and deer skins. Some wore feathered headdresses.

Chapter 5—Great Basin Indians

The tribes that were part of the Great Basin Indians lived in parts of Idaho, Wyoming, Colorado, Utah and Nevada. The Great Basin is a very dry area.

The Indians who lived in the Great Basin had to travel to hunt and gather their food. They built houses called ``wickiups'' out of willow poles covered with brush and grass.

Some Indians became very important people. A famous Great Basin Indian, named Sacajawea helped guide the explorers, Lewis and Clark. She was a Shoshone Indian.

Chapter 6—The Plateau Indians

The tribes that were part of the Plateau Indians lived in parts of Washington, Oregon, Idaho and Montana. The plateau is dry.

In the winter, Plateau Indians lived by the rivers and fished for salmon. When the warm weather came, they moved from the river area onto the plains to hunt and gather food.

The Plateau Indians had to have houses that were easy to move. Some of their houses were made of woven mats and poles.

Chapter 7—Northwest Coastal Indians

The tribes that were part of the Northwest Coastal Indians lived along the Pacific Ocean. These Indians got most of their food from the ocean.

There was a lot of rain where they lived and great forests grew there. The Northwest Indians used the trees in many ways. They built fine houses. They carved totem poles and masks. They carved cedar chests. Some Northwest tribes made beautiful blankets from wool and cedar bark.

Chapter 8—Southwest Indians

The tribes that were part of the Southwest Indians lived in Arizona and New Mexico. It is very dry there. It can be very hot there too.

One Southwest tribe was called the Apaches. The Apaches hunted and gathered their food. A famous Apache chief was Geronimo. He was a fighter and led many battles.

Since they had to move to find food they lived in houses that could be moved. They called their houses "wickiups."

The other tribes in the Southwest were farmers and craftsmen. They didn't move around so they built large apartment like buildings. Some of these homes had no windows or doors on the ground level. After they were inside, they would pull their ladders up so no one else could get into the house. Their homes were called ``pueblos or adobes.'' Southwest Indians are also well known for their pottery and baskets.

Chapter 9—Native Americans

There are many differences in the Indian tribes from around the United States, but there are also many things that are the same. Native Americans are a very interesting group of people.

There are still many tribes of Native Americans today, living in different parts of the United States. You can read more about them by looking for books on Native Americans or Indians in your school or city library.

SOCIAL ISSUES AND CULTURE

ACCEPTANCE

A Frog a Fly and a Friend

My name is Tom. This is my friend José. I like to say, ''Hey José.'' My friend, José is just learning English.

Once he said, "Oh look, a frog! There is a frog on the window."

It was not a frog. It was a fly.

Everybody laughed. José felt shy.

Our teacher showed him a picture of a frog.

"This is a frog," she said. "And that is called a fly."

Then José laughed, too.

I like José.

Now sometimes when I see a picture of a frog I say, "Hey José! There is a fly in my book." Then we laugh and laugh.

Kate and her friends looked out the window. It was raining. It had been raining all day.

``I wish we could go outside,'' she said.

``I wish we could play soccer,'' said Carlos.

``I wish we could play basketball,'' said Mimi.

``I wish we could play basketball, too,'' said Josh.

The others looked at Josh, sitting in his wheelchair.

``I didn't know you could play basketball,'' said Carlos.

``Sure,'' said Josh. ``I play all the time. I play with some other kids in wheelchairs. The rules are a little different, but we really have fun.''

``You never told us that before,'' said Mimi.

``You never asked,'' said Josh. ``I like to swim, too. But I like horseback riding the best.''

``Horseback riding!'' said Kate and Carlos together.

Josh nodded. ``I go horseback riding every week. Sometimes I ride a horse called Penny. Sometimes I ride Rob Roy. It's more fun than anything.''

"I've never been on a horse," said Kate.

"When I ride a horse," said Josh, "I feel as if I'm on top of the world."

Kate grinned at Josh.

"Could we watch you ride sometime?" asked Carlos.

"Of course," said Josh. "Come anytime."

"Really?" asked Mimi, her eyes shining.

``Hey, look,'' said Carlos. He pointed toward the window. ``The rain has stopped!''

``We can go outside,'' said Kate.

``We can play basketball,'' said Carlos. ``Josh, will you teach us your rules?''

``Sure!'' said Josh.

Mimi opened the door. ``Then let's go!''

Why People Immigrate

When people immigrate, they leave their country and go to live in another country. People immigrate for many different reasons.

Long, long ago the Pilgrims left England and immigrated to America. They wanted a better life. Everyone who immigrates wants a better life. They want better houses, plenty of food, and happiness. They want freedom to be what they want to be.

Johnny came to America from Ireland. He came a long time ago. Johnny came because everybody in Ireland was hungry. The poor people only had potatoes to eat. One year the potato crop was bad. There were no potatoes to eat, so Johnny and many others left Ireland. They immigrated to America.

Lucy was born in a small village in Mexico. She had big dreams. She wanted a good job. But there were no jobs in her small village, so Lucy and many others left that village. Some of them immigrated to America.

Thad was born in Poland. Poland was not free when Thad grew up. People could not say what they wanted. They could not go to church if they wanted. Thad wanted to live in a free country, so Thad and many others immigrated to America.

It is not easy to leave your country. Only brave people immigrate to a new country. Many times they must leave family and friends. In the new country they must learn new ways. But many people have done it. Many people have immigrated to America.

The Smallest Clown in the CIRCUS

Suzy was a clown. She was a very, very small clown. She was the smallest clown in the circus.

Suzy was a sad clown too. The bigger clowns teased her a lot. They were not being mean. They were just having fun. But the teasing made Suzy feel bad.

``I wish I were bigger,'' she sighed.

The bigger clowns would not let Suzy play a <u>big</u> part during the circus shows.

``You are too small!'' they said. ``Wait until you are bigger.''

Suzy spent a lot of time with the circus dogs that dressed like clowns. She fed them and played with them. She dressed the dogs for the shows. She even helped them practice their tricks. Suzy wished she could have a little part with the dogs during the shows. But the bigger clowns said, "You are too small! Wait until you are bigger."

One day, three of the bigger clowns were sick. They could not do the show with the clown dogs. But no one told Suzy. She dressed the dogs for their tricks and sent them into the circus ring.

The clown dogs ran into the center ring. Then they stopped. They looked at each other. They looked at the people in the stands. They were not sure what to do.

Then Suzy ran into the ring. She wanted to get the dogs out of there and back into their pens.

The clown dogs saw Suzy. They began doing their tricks. Suzy decided to let them stay in the ring. She helped the clown dogs with their act.

The clown dogs walked on their hind legs. They rolled barrels around the ring. They jumped through hoops. The audience clapped. They cheered. They cried out for more.

Finally, the clown dogs were finished. The ringmaster bellowed over the microphone, ``That was Suzy the smallest clown in the circus, with her trained clown dogs! Suzy, take another bow!''

Suzy ran back into the center ring. She turned cartwheels from one side to the other. The crowd loved her!

``I don't have to be big,'' Suzy grinned. ``There is nothing wrong with being the smallest clown in the circus.''

The Letter Q

Once upon a time, a long time ago, there was a sad little letter. This letter was known as **Q**. **Q** was sad because it was different from the other letters.

How was it different? Well, **Q** needed the help of U in order to spell a word. Without **U**'s help, no one could read what **Q** wrote. The words just looked odd—

Qick, **Q**een, **Q**iet.

Do you see what I mean?

So, U helped. Whenever **Q** began a word, **U** stood next to it to help spell the word—

Quick, **Qu**een, **Qu**iet!!

With **Q** leaning on **U**, it could spell many words.

But needing the help of another letter all the time made **Q** feel odd. It was afraid that the other letters laughed at it behind its back.

So, early one day, of that long ago year,

Q decided to leave the rest of the alphabet.

Well, the other letters noticed right away that **Q** was gone. Words like—

UEEN and UIET

just didn't make sense.

ABCDE
FGHIJ
KLMNO
P RST
UVWXY
Z

And when anybody tried to sing the "Alphabet Song," there was a hole.

All the letters agreed that they were just not complete without Q.

They searched high

and

low

UNTIL . . .

They finally found the letter **Q**.

The other alphabet letters told **Q** how much it had been missed. **X** told **Q** that each letter is different in some way, but they were all needed.

When it saw how much it was needed and wanted, **Q** came back to the alphabet.

Thank goodness, or you would not be able to

QUIT reading this story.

BIBLIOGRAPHY FOR THE SELECTION, A LOOK AT LIZARDS

A First Look at Snakes, Lizards, and Other Reptiles, Millicent E. Selsam and Joyce Hunt, Walker and Co., New York, 1975.

Lizard Tails and Cactus Spines, Barbara Brenner, Harper and Row, New York, 1975.

Reptiles Do The Strangest Things, Leonora and Arthur Hornblow, Random House, 1970.

The World of Lizards, Virginia Harrison, Garth Publishing, Milwaukee, Wis., 1988.